You would bless me indeed, and enlarge my territory
keep me from evil, that I may not cause pain!" So God
God of Israel, saying, "Oh, that You would bless me
with me, and that You would keep me from evil, that
And Jabez called on the God of Israel, saying, "Oh,
that Your hand would be with me, and that You would
wanted him what he requested. And Jabez called on
and enlarge my territory, that Your hand would be w
not cause pain!" So God granted him what he requested

To:

From:

that You would bless me indeed, and enlarge my terri
keep me from evil, that I may not cause pain!" So G
God of Israel, saying, "Oh, that You would bless
with me, and that You would keep me from evil, that
And Jabez called on the God of Israel, saying, "O
that Your hand would be with me, and that You wo
wanted him what he requested. And Jabez called on
and enlarge my territory that Your hand would be w

Jabez called on the God of Israel, saying, "Oh, that You would bless me indeed, and enlarge my territory, that Your hand would be with me, and that You would keep me from evil, that I may not cause pain!" So God granted him what he requested. And Jabez called on the God of Israel, saying, "Oh, that You would bless me indeed, and enlarge my territory, that Your hand would be with me, and that You would keep me from evil, that I may not cause pain!" So God granted him what he requested. And Jabez called on the God of Israel, saying, "Oh, that You would bless me indeed, and enlarge my territory, that Your hand would be with me, and that You would keep me from evil, that I may not cause pain!" So God granted him what he requested. And Jabez called on the God of Israel, saying, "Oh, that You would bless me indeed, and enlarge my territory, that Your hand would be with me, and that You would keep me from evil, that I may not cause pain!"

And Jabez Called on God...

BLESSINGS FOR ABUNDANCE IN EVERYDAY LIFE

By Sarah M. Hupp

INSPIRE

*With special thanks to Ginny, Elizabeth,
and Evie; and to Friskie, who truly believes
that "more things are wrought by prayer
than this world dreams of" (Tennyson).*

Inspire Books is an imprint of
Peter Pauper Press, Inc.

For permissions, please see the last page of this book.

Designed by Heather Zschock

Visit us at www.peterpauper.com

Contents

The Prayer 5

Introduction 6

A Life of Integrity 10

A Blessed Existence 16

A Way to Grow 32

The Presence of God 49

God's Caring Way 60

He Answers Prayer 70

And Jabez called on the God of Israel saying, "Oh, th[at]
You would bless me indeed, and enlarge my territory, th[at]
Your hand would be with me, and that You would ke[ep]
[m]e from evil, that I may not cause pain!" So God gran[ted]
[t]him what he requested. And Jabez called on the G[od]
[of] Israel saying, "Oh, that You would bless me indee[d]
[a]nd enlarge my territory, that Your hand would be wi[th]
[m]e, and that You would keep me from evil, that I m[ay]
[n]ot cause pain!" So God granted him what [he]
[re]quested. And Jabez called on the God of Israel sa[y]
[in]g, "Oh, that You would bless me indeed, and enlarge [my]
[te]rritory, that Your hand would be with me, and that Y[ou]
[w]ould keep me from evil, that I may not cause pain!" S[o]
[G]od granted him what he requested. And Jabez call[ed]
[o]n the God of Israel saying, "Oh, that You would ble[ss]
[m]e indeed, and enlarge my territory, that Your hand wou[ld]
[be] with me, and that You would keep me from evil, th[at]

The Prayer of Jabez

Now Jabez was more honorable than
his brothers, and his mother called
his name Jabez, saying, "Because
I bore him in pain." And Jabez called
on the God of Israel, saying,
"Oh, that You would bless me indeed,
and enlarge my territory,
that Your hand would be with me,
and that You would keep me from evil,
that I may not cause pain!"
So God granted him what he requested.

1 CHRONICLES 4:9-10 NKJV

5

Introduction

In the midst of a recitation of unfamiliar names with forgotten faces a human drama unfolds, granting us a glimpse of a man whose prayer took him from anonymity and pain to recognition and reward. This Bible hero was a simple man named Jabez.

Although Jabez lived centuries ago, the lessons he learned and lived are

timeless gems hidden within a few lines of the Old Testament. An honorable man, Jabez prayed specifically for God's blessings, recognizing God's immediate willingness to grant his requests for protection, prosperity, and God's presence.

One night not long ago, the adult members of the Spencer family sat around the kitchen table discussing family

matters. Sue shared with the others her concern for her husband's joblessness.

Sue's brother suggested that the family pray and ask God to help Bill find a job, but Sue frowned. "God's too busy taking care of more important things like floods and famine," she said. "He doesn't have time to care about small things like Bill's job."

Jabez would disagree. He wasn't afraid to ask God for anything, big or little. The

Bible tells us that God blessed Jabez abundantly, giving him everything he asked for.

God has time to hear your prayers, too. His blessings are available for you just as they were for Jabez. And those blessings may be only a prayer away.

A Life of Integrity

❖ IT SHALL BE GIVEN ❖

Jesus said: "Ask, and it shall be given you."

MATTHEW 7:7 KJV

While working in South Africa, Ginny met a missionary couple who ministered to the inhabitants of the Namibian desert. The missionaries had established a nutrition program, a mission school, and a

Sunday school, too. Occasionally the couple would come to the city for supplies, sometimes stopping to see Ginny.

On one such visit, the missionary couple told a miraculous tale. Because of a series of mishaps, the couple had not received their monthly stipend. They had run out of food. Yet, without money, they couldn't buy supplies in the city. Their other resources were limited, too, so they had no means to trade with the local people.

Their only recourse was prayer. Calmly, confidently, they asked God to send them food. And God did just that. Shortly after the missionaries had finished praying, a local farmer drove up in his battered truck and began to unload parcels of fresh game. He and his sons had shot much more than they needed, so the farmer had brought the leftovers to the missionaries.

As the couple related their tale, Ginny was amazed at their faith in God's willingness to supply their need. They didn't worry whether God would hear or answer. They took Him at His word: "Ask, and it shall be given you."

They asked. Have you?

Jabez was more honorable than his brothers.

1 CHRONICLES 4:9 NASB

Jabez lived his life with integrity and godliness, recognizing that greatness comes not by personal advantage, but rather through God's power. As the South African missionaries learned, God will send blessings to all of his children, but especially to those who recognize how much they need Him.

Thou art coming to a King,
Large petitions with thee bring
For His grace and power are such
None can ever ask too much.

JOHN NEWTON

A Blessed Existence

The LORD will guard your going
out and your coming in
From this time forth and forever.

PSALM 121:8 NASB

Sixteen-year-old Elsa and her cousin Mari
were ready to leave their home in Riga,
Latvia, to visit relatives in the United

States. The journey would take weeks, with travel across thousands of miles until their final arrival in New York City. Before the girls left home they prayed with Elsa's father for safety, health, and good weather.

What an adventure for the two cousins! They marveled at the beauty of Stockholm and Copenhagen and laughed at the antics of street performers in Liverpool. But four days before they were to leave England, Mari came down with

flu-like symptoms. Doctors refused to grant her an exit visa.

Bitterly disappointed, Elsa went to the dockside ticket office to explain their predicament. The ticket agent cheerfully issued the cousins two tickets for the next ship heading for America, informing Elsa that there would be no additional charge since he was very sure he could resell their current berths. It seemed that everyone was clamoring to sail aboard the White

Star Line's finest ship.

The flu-like symptoms. The refusal of an exit visa. Two minor inconveniences that ultimately saved my grandmother Elsa's life. For the cousins, you see, had originally been booked on the Titanic. The seemingly inconsequential prayer of a worried father for a daughter's travels held the key to providence and protection. Because of God's gracious answer to that father's prayer, I am alive today!

❖ A PLACE TO CALL HOME ❖

And the Lord will continually guide you.

ISAIAH 58:11 NASB

A Colorado Bible college sent two young women to Tokyo, Japan to teach English classes. When they arrived, the two women began praying for a place to live. Yet, as time drew near for them to start

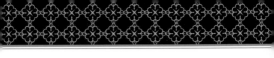

classes, they still had not found a suitable dwelling. Local landlords were reluctant to rent to strangers.

Despite this setback, the two teachers decided to familiarize themselves with the city. While traversing the maze of twisting streets, they became lost. Looking about for a street sign, they noticed a photo of a house in a store window. A sign above the photo said merely, "Inquire inside."

Intrigued, the two women entered the shop and asked about the photo in the window. The shopkeeper replied that the house was too big for most Japanese families, and he had been having trouble renting it. When asked where it was located, the man gave an address that was close to the teachers' new school.

Minutes later, the teachers left the shop carrying a copy of a signed lease agreement. The home met their needs

exactly—convenient to shopping and
trains, and near their school and contacts.
God had truly found them a place to
call home.

✦ CONSTITUTIONAL CHAOS ✦

Unless the Lord builds the house,
its builders labor in vain.

PSALM 127:1 NIV

On a recent trip to Philadelphia, Pennsylvania, our family toured Carpenter's Hall. We listened attentively to park rangers who regaled us with tales about the framers of our constitution. Among the pieces of trivia they shared, a story

about prayer took center stage.

History records that the Constitutional
Convention of 1787 was deadlocked. At
issue was a battle between the smaller
states and the larger ones over each one's
representation in government. Heated
debates had continued all day when
Benjamin Franklin finally took the floor.

This elder statesman knew that only
God could foster the needed compromise.
"Gentlemen," he said, "I . . . am convinced

that God governs in the affairs of men. If a sparrow cannot fall to the ground without His notice, is it probable that an empire can rise without His aid? I move that prayer imploring the assistance of Heaven be held every morning before we proceed to business."

Franklin's motion was carried without debate. Each morning thereafter, a prayer was offered, invoking God's guidance in the delegates' affairs. Remarkably, attitudes

began to reflect the more peaceable atmosphere, and, within a few short days, a dramatic compromise was reached that is still in effect in our Congressional houses today. God's answer to those delegates' prayers set the course for the future of our country.

❧ GOOD GIFTS ❧

*How much more your heavenly Father will
give good things to those who ask him!*

MATTHEW 7:11 NCV

Have you ever driven through a crowded
parking lot on a rainy day, praying for a
parking spot near the door—and then
actually found one? Have you ever secretly
wished for something wonderful to happen, and then, unexpectedly, it happened?

Some folks may say these occurrences
are mere coincidences or accidents of
nature. Others, like Jabez, would see God's
hand of blessing in these serendipities.

When Jabez prayed for God's blessing, he literally was asking God to lead
him, strengthen him, and work out all
things in and for his good.

God, by nature, is beneficent, gracious, and loving. Much as a doting grand-
parent hears the longing in a grandchild's

wish for some trinket, so God hears our sighs for things like parking spaces and good weather. And, sometimes, unexpectedly, God grants those whispered prayers.

There's no secret formula to guarantee your wish will come true, for God is not a genie in a bottle. But you never know when there just might be an outpouring of God's love to answer your wistful prayer and guarantee your grateful smile in return.

> *Oh, that You would bless me indeed.*
>
> 1 CHRONICLES 4:10 NKJV

Some assume God does not like to be troubled with personal requests. In reality, the way to trouble God is not to come to Him at all. God wasn't disturbed by Jabez's request for a life filled with blessings; He graced Jabez with all he had requested. By Jabez's example, we, too, can freely ask for God's best in all areas of our lives and find His blessings in abundance.

A Way to Grow

◈ PEANUT PROSPERITY ◈

*You, Lord, have never forsaken
those who seek you.*

PSALM 9:10 NIV

A little-known story about the southeast-
ern corner of Alabama clearly illustrates
God's willingness to answer prayer. This
primarily agricultural region of the state

used to be blanketed with cotton fields. But in 1915 an invasion of boll weevils threatened those fields.

Farmers and their families met for prayer, asking God to spare their crops and help them provide for their families. But the weevils continued their destruction, eventually consuming more than 60% of the cotton in that one-crop area.

Families were devastated. Hadn't God heard their prayers?

Some of the farmers banded together, asking God for help again. News reports of some unusual research by a Christian botanist in Tuskegee intrigued them. So, the next growing season, these farmers followed George Washington Carver's advice and successfully planted a new crop—peanuts. The following season, other farmers followed their lead and planted peanuts, too.

Within two years, these farmers were earning more money per acre from peanuts than they had ever earned from their fields of cotton.

God *had* heard the farmers' prayers, but He had answered in an unexpected way. Instead of restoring a former way of life, God had blended the work of a struggling botanist with the prayers of a few farmers and paved the way for abundant blessings in Coffee County, Alabama.

◈ A BETTER PERSPECTIVE ◈

You will come to me and pray to me,
and I will listen to you.

JEREMIAH 29:12 NCV

The airplane rose swiftly to its cruising altitude, carrying me across the country to an important meeting. The responsibilities of a growing family, aging parents, and a

fledgling business pulled at me from all angles, fragmenting my thoughts and confronting me with endless problems that needed immediate resolution.

Tears trickled down my cheeks as I silently poured my heart out in prayer to God. I couldn't take any more. Something had to change. My personal problems loomed so large, they threatened to obscure the sun that beamed through the cabin window.

I glanced out and caught a glimpse of the landscape far below. We were flying over the Rocky Mountains, over terrain that took hours to traverse in an automobile. Yet as we whooshed along at 20,000 feet, those mountains resembled a succession of wrinkles that were left far behind in a matter of minutes.

I shifted in my seat and bumped elbows with another passenger. Apologizing for disturbing her, I noticed her hands were clutching a Bible. Her face was damp with perspiration. "Are you all right?" I inquired gently. Her nervous nod and desperate look said volumes.

She spoke haltingly of an ailing mother. She was unsure whether she would arrive in time to say her last goodbye. I suggested we pray together. As we prayed, I noticed that she stopped twisting her handkerchief. A calmness pervaded her being.

The view outside my window had
changed a bit during our moments of
prayer, but my insight had expanded
immensely. Just as my seatmate's fears had
been allayed, I realized that I, too, had
found a different perspective to help me
face my problems.

Because I had been focusing too
closely on my circumstances, my life had
seemed as troublesome to navigate as an
automobile trek through the Rockies.

I had been blinded to God's greatness, had forgotten His goodness, and had neglected His willingness to come to our aid.

But prayer, and a chat with my seatmate, reminded me that I could view life from a different perspective. In God's eyes, my problems were mere wrinkles in life's fabric. With Him in control, I could soar above the problems without worry or fear.

Oh, what a blessing that flight over the mountains became! When my heart

had cried, "Help!" God was there in an instant—showing me a better perspective, reminding me of His blessings, and assuring me of His abiding concern. With a whispered prayer of gratitude, I closed my eyes and slept.

❖ WHEN TWO AGREED ❖

If two of you on earth agree about
anything you ask for, it will be done
for you by my Father in heaven.

MATTHEW 18:19 NIV

One Sunday the pastor in a Mississippi
delta town quoted Matthew 18:19 in his
sermon. After the service, as he greeted
parishioners at the door, a poor woman

asked him quietly, "Does God really mean that if two of us pray, it will happen?"

The pastor quickly assured her that indeed the promise of Scripture was true. Pressing her point, the woman continued, "Will you pray with me, Reverend?"

The pastor knew immediately what the poor woman wanted, for her husband was a renowned reprobate, a foul-mouthed fisherman who spent Sunday mornings sleeping off his nights

of drinking and carousing.

A student behind them spoke up. "I'll pray with you, ma'am," he said. The young man ushered the woman to a corner of the vestibule, where they began to pray for her husband.

Later that evening the church opened its doors for a song festival. The pastor was astonished to see the woman come down the center aisle, accompanied by her unshaven husband and the young student.

The curious trio took the last seats available.

At the close of the musical presentation, while the pastor invited those who desired God's touch to come to the podium, the woman and the student prayed. And God answered their prayers, for the foul-mouthed fisherman was one of the first to respond to the pastor's call.

Thereafter, though the fisherman continued to frequent the bars and brothels,

he no longer went to drink or carouse, but rather to share how God had changed his life when two had believed God's promise and prayed for him.

Oh, that You would . . .
enlarge my territory.

1 CHRONICLES 4:10 NKJV

When Jabez asked God to enlarge his territory, his request encompassed more than just acquiring additional real estate. Jabez realized our experiences limit us, our habits confine us, but change offers us a way to grow. Whether we face a career change, a changed perspective, or a changed life, we can pray in faith, trusting God to enlarge our territory and release us to be more than we ever dreamt possible.

The Presence of God

❖ A QUIET HEART ❖

Be still, and know that I am God.

PSALM 46:10 KJV

I read the Psalmist's admonition before falling asleep last night: "Be still, and know that I am God." What a peaceful thought—finding stillness and discovering God.

Yet this morning the clock-radio blasted me awake with an announcer's clipped delivery of fast-breaking news stories. In the next room, our teenager's stereo began its 18-hour job of filling nearby ears with the latest sounds from the music store. Noises from the street—growling mufflers, honking horns, and blaring sirens—poured through the open windows.

I stumbled to the kitchen, hoping for

a respite from the noise, but was greeted instead with a whirring refrigerator that seemed to be talking to the clanking air conditioner. As I added the drip, drip, sploosh of the coffeemaker to the morning's din, I recalled that Phillips Brooks once wrote, "Prayer, in its simplest definition, is merely a wish turned God-ward."

"All right," I said aloud. "If you want me to be still, God, *I wish you'd help!*" With a thump, I plopped down on a

chair, clasping my steaming mug of caffeine. Abruptly the deep, bass notes of our teen's stereo ceased, choked out of existence. As I blinked in amazement, our young rock-star appeared in the kitchen doorway, muttering something about a blown speaker.

I proffered my steaming mug and patted the chair next to me. For the next fifteen minutes we sat and talked in the relative quiet, sharing together like old

friends, our words interweaving observations with insight and laughter. All too soon the moment ended, and we parted ways to start our day.

As I stepped into the shower, I realized that my heart was quiet. In the midst of all the racket of a busy morning, the blessing of a loved one's presence and the shared remembrance of simple joys had washed stillness over my soul. Surrounded by the sounds of the morning, I had

found not only an answer to my prayer,
but a sense of God's presence and an
added blessing of closeness with my child.

✤ A HEAVENLY CONCERT ✤

The hearing ear and the seeing eye,
The Lord has made both of them.

PROVERBS 20:12 NASB

The elderly couple had been married for over fifty years when cancer claimed the beloved husband unexpectedly. Perplexed and troubled, the new widow realized she had lost not only her soulmate, but her ears, too.

Because her hearing loss could not be improved with hearing aids, she had depended on her husband to listen for the doorbell or to respond to a visitor's questions. Now that she faced the task of coping with her hearing loss alone, she asked God for reassurance that everything would be all right.

As the family gathered at the cemetery, the widow strained to hear the pastor's reassuring words, but heard

nothing. Traffic rushed by in the street
below, but her ears never heard its passing.

Yet when the pastor began to describe
the joyous music of Heaven, the family
noticed a strange sound, sweet and clear.
Above the din of traffic, a chorus of birds
could be heard. The widow's face broke
into a smile. At the final "Amen" she
asked excitedly, "Did you hear the birds?
Weren't they beautiful?" The family was
amazed. How could one so deaf have

heard such a gentle sound? Before their
eyes her anxiety dissolved, her shoulders
relaxed, and she felt a peace and content-
ment only God can give. Joyfully the
widow declared, "If God can help these
old ears hear His birds, He can take care
of the rest of my needs, too."

Oh . . . that Your hand would be with me.

1 CHRONICLES 4:10 NKJV

Jabez asked for God's hand to stay with him, a request for God's presence in every aspect of his life. Jabez knew that there would be no safety, no clarity of vision, no decisive direction without God. Our needs are no different today. Yet formal prayers are unnecessary. A sigh, a whisper, a murmur—all signal a cry of the heart for His presence; all find their way to God.

God's Caring Way

He makes the clouds His chariot;
He walks upon the wings of the wind.

PSALM 104:3 NASB

During World War II, American bomb
assaults in the Pacific theater sometimes
originated from the island of Guam. It was
common practice for the base chaplains to

conduct prayer services prior to the bombing runs. God's protection was invoked, for both the pilots and their crews and for innocent victims who might stray into harm's way.

An early morning strike was ordered for Kokura, Japan. The chaplain gathered the men together for a few moments of silent prayer. Heads bowed as each man asked for God's blessing.

The squadron of bombers took off

and streaked toward their target, heavily laden with deadly cargo. Kokura, their primary objective, was obscured by dense fog and clouds. The aviators waited tensely for a break in the overcast sky.

After holding this attack pattern for almost an hour, the squadron was ordered to head for a secondary target. Upon arrival at the new site, the bombers found the sky clear, released their cargo, and headed for home.

Weeks later an ashen-faced intelligence officer approached the Guam base commander. He held out a report with shaky hands, stammering, "Remember that run to Kokura, sir? The one with the heavy clouds? It seems that a week before we made that run the Japanese had turned Kokura into a prison camp. If we had completed that run, sir, thousands of our boys would have been killed. Thank God for those clouds!"

Thank God, indeed. Our prayers for protection have far-reaching consequences. God's intervention on our behalf may involve a small change of events or a major change in the weather. But when He does intervene, thank God.

✦ GUARDED BY GOD ✦

You are my hiding place;
you will protect me from trouble.

PSALM 32:7 NIV

The car rolled once onto its roof and
screeched to a halt almost thirty feet down
the highway. Shattered glass littered the
lone occupant hanging upside down from
her seat belt, but the state trooper who
called our home that night assured us that

our daughter would be fine.

Sending a child off to college hundreds of miles away from home is never easy. But though our oldest child was no longer under our roof, she was never out of our prayers. Daily we requested God's guidance in her relationships and her studies. Daily we petitioned God for her safekeeping. And God was listening.

At the auto impound the day after the accident, our daughter found her vehicle,

its roof crushed to within inches of the
steering wheel. Visibly shaken, she opened
the trunk and gasped with amazement. A
small item had sifted to the top and center
of the trunk's jumbled contents—a color-
ful sticker that boldly proclaimed, "Angels
watching over me!"

The sticker's message spoke resound-
ingly to our daughter of God's answer to
our prayers for her safety. Though hundreds of miles might have separated us

from each other that terrifying night, a dime-store sticker was there to remind us that our eldest was never separated from God's blessing of protection.

> *Keep me from evil.*
>
> 1 CHRONICLES 4:10 NKJV

Jabez trusted God to keep him from all kinds of harm—from the trouble of sin, danger, and the evil designs of his enemies. God granted Jabez his request and blessed him with deliverance, safety, and security. These rich blessings are available to us, too, if we but ask God to enfold us in His strong, protective arms.

He Answers Prayer

Remember the Lord your God,
for it is he who gives you the
ability to produce wealth.

DEUTERONOMY 8:18 NIV

It had happened again. We had come to
the end of the paycheck before we came
to the end of the month. It seemed like it

was written in stone somewhere: As long as you have children living at home, you'll always have more month than money.

My husband and I had reviewed our budget numerous times and felt we were on the right track to setting some money aside for the future. But unexpected emergencies seemed to sneak up on us and rob us of those extra nickels and dimes. We agreed it was time to take another approach.

Anyone peering through our windows that October morning would have been greeted with a strange sight. There we were, my husband and I, our heads bowed over a Mason jar full of credit card slips, overdue bills, and a "must-do" list, offering a heartfelt plea for God's blessing on our finances. Yet, the final "Amen" brought a sense that all would be well.

Weeks later, when the calendar flipped past October 31, we found we had finished the month in the black. How had this happened? To this day we're not sure. Whether God held back a few emergencies in that five-week month or gifted us with a miracle, one thing is certain: He had heard our prayers. God had helped us stretch our pennies where we had been unable to do it alone. And He can do it for you, too.

❖ GOD'S UNPREDICTABILITY ❖

Call to Me, and I will answer you,
and I will tell you great and mighty things,
which you do not know.

JEREMIAH 33:3 NASB

Of one thing there's no doubt—God
answers prayer! How He will do it is
another matter. God may give you what
you pray for, or He may give you something even better. Often God's answers to

our prayers come in unpredictable ways.

The Bible tells us in Acts 16 that Paul
and Silas were chained in a Philippian
prison. Prayers were offered for immediate
deliverance. Yet God left the situation
unchanged, changing instead the men's
attitude toward their circumstances. Their
faithful prayers and songs of hope touched
guards and fellow prisoners, so that when
finally they were released, many lives had
been blessed.

Joshua 7 records the defeat of the Israelites at Ai. Joshua bemoaned this loss, petitioning God for strength and victory. But God did not offer him comfort or assurance. Rather, God gruffly instructed Joshua to rouse the people to penitence. The people themselves held the key to God's blessings, for their earlier disobedience had brought about their present defeat. By changing the course of their own actions, success could be theirs again.

Yet there are times when God chose to alter a bad situation. When Peter was bound between two guards in Herod's prison, Acts 12 records that God delivered him from his chains and escorted him through the city to safety.

God may be unpredictable in the way He works for our good, but of one thing there's no doubt—God answers prayer. You can count on it!

> *So God granted him what he requested.*
>
> 1 CHRONICLES 4:10 NKJV

Cursed with a name that means "pain," Jabez trusted God to work out everything in his life for good. The sorrow implied by Jabez's ill-omened name was averted by the blessing of answered prayer. Sometimes we are so intent on forecasting the way God will answer our prayers, we don't recognize His answers when they do